The Plymouth Colony

Janet Riehecky

WORLD ALMANAC® LIBRARY

Please visit our web site at: www.worldalmanaclibrary.com
For a free color catalog describing World Almanac® Library's list of high-quality
books and multimedia programs, call 1-800-848-2928 (USA) or 1-800-387-3178
(Canada). World Almanac® Library's fax: (414) 332-3567.

Library of Congress Cataloging-in-Publication Data

Riehecky, Janet, 1953-
    The Plymouth Colony / by Janet Riehecky.
        p. cm. — (Landmark events in American history)
    Summary: Describes the establishment of the English colony at Plymouth,
Massachusetts, from its planning phase to the 1620 transatlantic journey of settlers,
as well as the experiences of those settlers in the new land.
    Includes bibliographical references and index.
    ISBN 0-8368-5340-7 (lib. bdg.)
    ISBN 0-8368-5354-7 (softcover)
    1. Massachusetts—History—New Plymouth, 1620-1691—Juvenile literature.
[1. Plymouth (Mass.)—History. 2. Massachusetts—History—New Plymouth, 1620-1691.
3. Pilgrims (New Plymouth Colony).] I. Title. II. Series.
F68.R54   2002
974.4'8202—dc21   2002024637

This North American edition first published in 2002 by
World Almanac® Library
330 West Olive Street, Suite 100
Milwaukee, WI 53212 USA

This U.S. edition © 2002 by World Almanac® Library.

Produced by Discovery Books
Editor: Sabrina Crewe
Designer and page production: Sabine Beaupré
Photo researcher: Sabrina Crewe
Maps and diagrams: Stefan Chabluk
World Almanac® Library editorial direction: Mark J. Sachner
World Almanac® Library art direction: Tammy Gruenewald
World Almanac® Library production: Susan Ashley

Photo credits: Boston City Council, U.K.: p. 10; Corbis: cover, pp. 4, 37, 42, 43; Granger
Collection: pp. 18, 19, 20, 22, 23, 38; Donald Hinds: pp. 6, 8, 24, 26, 30, 32, 34; North
Wind Picture Archives: pp. 5, 7, 9, 11, 12, 13, 14, 16, 17, 21, 25, 27, 28, 29, 31, 36, 39,
40, 41; Pilgrim Society and Pilgrim Hall Museum: p. 33.

Printed in the United States of America

1 2 3 4 5 6 7 8 9 06 05 04 03 02

Contents

Introduction

Near the town of Plymouth in Massachusetts, a reconstruction has been built of the original village as it probably looked in 1627. It is called Plimoth Plantation, and this is a view looking down the main street to the sea.

On September 16, 1620, a sailing ship named the *Mayflower* left England for North America. It carried about one hundred people, including a number of **Puritan Separatists** looking for a place where they could build a new community based on their religious beliefs. The journey was a difficult and dangerous one, and it was the middle of winter before the passengers on the *Mayflower* found a site to settle. Nonetheless, the travelers soon founded the **colony** of Plymouth in what is now Massachusetts.

Puritans and Separatists

England was a Catholic country until 1533. That year, King Henry VIII broke with the Catholic Church and formed the Church of England. Many reforms were made, but some people thought even more changes were needed to distance the Church of England further from the practices of the Catholics.

King James I ruled England from 1603 to 1625. He insisted that all Englishmen acknowledge him as their religious leader, and he did not follow the teachings of the Bible exactly, as some Christians felt should be done. These Christians wanted to "purify" the church and were known as Puritans. Most Puritans stayed in the Church of England, trying to reform it from within. Others, the Separatists, were **dissenters** who separated from the Church of England altogether. They would acknowledge no one as their spiritual leader except God. They believed the Bible, not the king, was the ultimate authority. A group of these Separatists left England during the reign of King James I and eventually settled in Plymouth.

Pilgrims

The settlers at Plymouth were referred to as "pilgrims" by William Bradford, governor of Plymouth for thirty years, in his book *Of Plimoth Plantation 1620–1647*, first published in full in 1856. In it, Bradford states, ". . .they knew they were pilgrims, and [did not look back] but lift[ed] up their eyes to the heavens, their dearest country, and quieted their spirits." The settlers at Plymouth did not call themselves pilgrims, however. The name was not commonly used to describe the Plymouth settlers until the nineteenth century, although it had been used before then to refer to any early European colonists.

The settlers at Plymouth—and other Puritans who arrived in North America after them—had a strong belief in the virtue of hard work. This "work ethic" became essential to Plymouth's survival and, later, an important value for many Americans. The colony was unlike other European settlements in North America, however, because, at first, the inhabitants worked for the common good, not just for individual gain.

The early colonists at Plymouth, or **Pilgrims** as they later came to be called, also had the first written **constitution** in North America. When they arrived, the people on the *Mayflower* wrote an agreement. It was called the "Mayflower **Compact**," and it proposed "just and equal" laws for governing the colony.

One of the first Plymouth colonists, Priscilla Mullins, steps ashore at Plymouth in 1620.

Chapter 1

New England's First Inhabitants

Wampanoag people of what is now New England were hunters as well as farmers. A Wampanoag man at Plimoth Plantation demonstrates here how his ancestors dried and decorated animal hides.

The Peoples of New England

Before the English colonists came to Massachusetts, about eighteen large Native groups and more than seventy-five smaller ones were living in the area now called New England. Recent estimates suggest that the Native population of New England totaled about 120,000 people in 1600.

The peoples in this area had similar lifestyles and spoke variations of the same Algonquian language. Each group was separate, but a smaller one might pay tribute to a larger, more powerful one. The most powerful group in the area was a **confederacy** of about fifty tribes, collectively called the Wampanoag. Estimates vary, but there were at least several thousand Wampanoag people in 1600. Other peoples in the area included Massachusets, Narragansetts, and Nausets.

Traditional Forms of Government

Within the Wampanoag Confederacy, the tribes had their own governments, each led by a sachem, or chief, and a council of advisors. A grand sachem had authority over all the other chiefs. The sachems' authority was limited, and they had to earn the respect of the group. The Wampanoag and their neighbors in New England did not have written laws but followed established customs enforced by public opinion. They would often spend a long time making decisions, trying to get everyone to agree. Most sachems were the descendants of previous sachems, and occasionally they were women.

Communal Life

Individuals did not own land in the Native societies of New England. Instead, groups claimed specific areas for their villages and farmland and widespread ranges for hunting and fishing. Most Wampanoag lived in villages near the coast in the summer months and moved inland during winter, living in family hunting camps. Hunting areas were clearly defined to avoid conflict, but some areas were open to any group.

These lodges were typical New England dwellings in the 1600s. Smaller than longhouses, they were built in the same way, with bark or straw mats laid over wooden saplings and poles.

Fish was an important food for the coastal New England peoples. This picture shows how fish was air dried to store for winter.

There were hundreds of villages scattered throughout the New England area, with an average of 250 inhabitants in each. Many villagers lived in longhouses with sides of bark and a rounded roof made of mats woven from reeds or other plants. There were no windows, just a door covered by a straw mat or animal skin. Each family had its own housing, and a family unit usually included extended family members such as grandparents and cousins.

Food Supply

In 1614, English explorer John Smith mapped the coastline of the area he named New England. He described the land as well-populated and planted with many gardens and noted that "The sea coast as you pass shews you all along large Corne fields." The Native people of New England were farmers who supplemented their food supply by hunting and fishing. Usually the women raised crops—such as corn, beans, and squash—and looked for berries, nuts, and other edible plants in the forests.

Seafood was the most reliable food available. There was a huge range in the Atlantic waters, where people caught—among other varieties—oysters, salmon, herring, and even turtles and whales. On land, men hunted anything from deer and bear to rabbits and pheasants, using animal scents and bird calls to lure prey into range. Hide and bones provided clothing, building materials, and tools.

Savage and Brutish

"The place they had thoughts on was some of those vast and unpeopled countries of America, which are fruitful and fit for habitation, being devoid [empty] of all civil inhabitants, where there are only savage and brutish men which range up and down, little otherwise than the wild beasts of the same."

William Bradford, governor of Plymouth Colony, describing what the colonists expected to find and offering a typical view of the English toward Native Americans, Of Plimoth Plantation 1620–1647

European Contact

The Native people of New England were generally taller, stronger, and healthier than their European counterparts in the 1600s. Like most other people across the North American continent, however, they did not stay healthy. Contact with European explorers had a devastating effect on the Indian nations. Explorers from Spain, England, and other European countries exposed North Americans to numerous diseases, such as measles, smallpox, and bubonic plague, to which they had no resistance.

Three epidemics between 1614 and 1620 raged throughout New England, devastating the Wampanoag among others. Thousands died, including sometimes the inhabitants of whole villages. In 1619, an English sailor, Captain Thomas Dermer, reported that the ancient settlements along the New England coast that had been populated by hundreds of people were now empty. The site of the future Plymouth colony was a good example. Just a few years before the colonists arrived, it had been occupied by Patuxet Wampanoags, but an **epidemic** wiped them out. The farmland and village of Patuxet were completely deserted.

Plans for a New Colony

In Search of Religious Freedom

In about 1606, a group of Christians in the English village of Scrooby formed their own Separatist church. This was considered a high crime by the English authorities, and the Separatists faced difficulties from the start. Some church members lost their jobs, some lost their possessions, and some were even imprisoned.

The Scrooby church members decided to leave England, even though it was against the law. Their destination was Holland, a province of the Netherlands where other Separatist groups had found religious freedom. At that time, the Netherlands was the only nation in Europe that permitted freedom of religion. By the summer of 1608, most of the Scrooby Separatists, about 125 people, had made it to Holland.

Life in the Netherlands

The Scrooby Separatists stayed a year in Amsterdam, the capital of the Netherlands, but there were too many disagreements with the other Separatist groups there for them to be comfortable. In 1609, they moved to the city of Leiden. There they faced other difficulties. At first, there was a language barrier because they couldn't speak Dutch, the national language. They also had difficulty keeping up their English traditions and customs, which were very important to them. Nearly all of the jobs available to the English involved hard labor for little pay.

As the years passed, the Separatists worried as their children married Dutch citizens and even joined the Dutch army. Above all, they worried that their Puritan values were being corrupted by the easygoing ways of the Dutch. And, finally, they worried because a treaty between Netherlands and Spain was about to end, and their religious freedom might be abolished if Catholic Spain took over the country.

A New World

Some of the Scrooby Separatists decided they should think about emigrating again, this time to the English colonies in North America, known to Europeans at that time as "the New World." There would be obstacles. They needed permission from the English authorities to settle there, and they had little money to pay the expenses.

In 1617, the Scrooby Separatists sent two agents to London to apply for a **patent** to settle in English North America. They approached the Virginia Company of London—or London Company—that had rights to land in North America and had already started a colony in Jamestown, Virginia. The London

The city of Leiden in the Netherlands, shown here, offered religious freedom to the Separatists from England, but it also offered their children a way of life that was not as strict as that of Puritan society. The Separatists began to look toward North America as a possible home.

Edward Winslow was a leading Separatist and among the first to emigrate to New England. He was instrumental in drawing up the Mayflower Compact and also one of the authors of *Mourt's Relation*, an account of early Plymouth. He later became assistant governor and then governor of the colony.

Company was eager to issue patents to settlers who would start farming colonies, but not to finance the colony. Plans stalled because the Separatists did not have enough money for the journey to North America nor to finance the colony themselves.

In 1619, a London businessman named Thomas Weston approached the Separatists as head of a group of people looking for an investment. Weston and the Separatists reached an agreement, and Weston supplied the money to gather the necessary supplies and equipment.

In February of 1620, the Scrooby Separatists received official permission to settle in the northern part of Virginia, a region that, at the time, extended north to the present state of New York.

Disagreements

The Scrooby Separatists had agreed that all profits from the colony for the first seven years would be split with the investors, but they wanted their individual homes and gardens excluded from this arrangement. They also wanted two days a week set aside for the men to work for themselves rather than for the colony. The investors did not want anything excluded from the profit sharing, however, and they wanted the men to work all seven days every week for the colony.

Robert Cushman and John Carver, the agents, agreed to the investors' terms and told the Scrooby Separatists that they had no choice in this if they wanted to get to America. The Separatists, however, refused to abide by the terms. Weston then withdrew his financial support, and the Separatists were forced to sell part of their provisions to raise the rest of the funds they needed to leave.

Departure

The Scrooby Separatists had bought a small ship, the *Speedwell*, to take them first to England and then to America. The emigration to America had divided the community, and the majority of church members decided to stay in Leiden. Only about thirty-five Separatists were making the voyage, although others planned to join the emigrants later.

On July 22, 1620, the *Speedwell* left the Netherlands for Southampton, England. There the travelers joined up with the *Mayflower*. Its passengers included other English Separatists and a group of non-Puritans. On August 5, 1620, the *Mayflower* and the *Speedwell* set sail from England.

The Departure from Leiden

". . . they went aboard and their friends with them, where truly doleful was the sight of that sad and mournful parting, to see what sighs and sobs and prayers did sound amongst them, what tears did gush from every eye. . . . And then with mutual embraces and many tears they took their leaves one of another, which proved to be the last leave to many of them."

William Bradford, Of Plimoth Plantation 1620–1647

After considerable expense and many setbacks, the group of thirty-five Scrooby Separatists left the Netherlands in July 1620. Because the majority were staying in Holland, the Scrooby pastor, John Robinson, shown center in black, stayed with them.

13

The Journey and Arrival

The *Mayflower* and the *Speedwell* didn't get far. Twice the travelers had to return to port because the *Speedwell* was leaking. With great reluctance, the leaders decided they would have to leave the *Speedwell* behind. Several men suspected the captain had deliberately sabotaged his own ship because he didn't want to make the journey to North America.

The *Mayflower* Sails Alone

Now that there was only one ship, some of the passengers had to stay in England. As many as possible, however, squeezed aboard the *Mayflower*. When it finally set sail from Plymouth, England, on September 16, 1620, the ship carried about one hundred passengers as well as its officers and crew. The passengers included the thirty-five members of the Scrooby Separatist Church and sixty-five to sixty-seven others, some of them "adventurers," or people who had

The *Mayflower* is tossed around on stormy waves during its journey across the Atlantic Ocean.

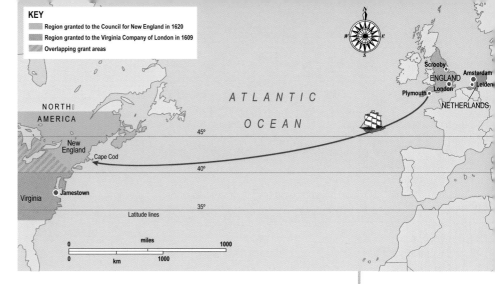

invested in the new colony. One of the non-Separatists, a soldier named Myles Standish, was appointed the colony's military commander. There were also a number of **indentured servants** and craftsmen. One of the crew members was a **cooper** named John Alden who, like several of the travelers, converted to Separatist Puritanism on the journey.

As the *Mayflower* progressed across the sea, it was buffeted by many storms. Some damaged the ship, and others forced it to drift wherever the wind blew it for days at a time. Sometimes there was no wind, and the passengers just sat and waited. During the voyage, a young servant named William Butten and one of the sailors died. One woman, Elizabeth Hopkins, gave birth to a boy, whom she named Oceanus.

The *Mayflower* traveled across the Atlantic from Europe to the east coast of North America. They landed in a region that was granted to the Council of New England in 1620. The region lay between 40° North (in present-day New Jersey) and 48° North (just above the present Canadian border).

The *Mayflower*

A small ship compared to those that cross the ocean today, the *Mayflower* would have been similar to other sailing ships of the time. Historians think it was about 100 feet (30 meters) long and about 25 feet (7 m) wide. It would have had three masts and two decks. The ship wasn't designed to hold as many people as actually made the journey. It had only primitive sanitary facilities and few cabins or bunks. Most of the passengers lived and slept in an area below deck that was dark and smelly with no place to wash clothes or take a bath. Along with its excessive number of passengers, the *Mayflower* was carrying a large amount of cargo in the form of fresh water, household items, food, and animals such as dogs, goats, and chickens.

The Wrong Place

On November 9, 1620, after two months at sea, the people on the *Mayflower* sighted land. The ship weighed anchor off what is now Provincetown Harbor in Cape Cod, Massachusetts, on November 11, 1620. This was north of their intended destination, which was the northernmost part of Virginia. The travelers knew they were not in Virginia but in a region that was claimed by King James I as "New England." Back in England—on November 13—this land was granted by the king to the Council of New England.

In the cabin of the *Mayflower*, a group of men, including Separatists, non-Separatists, and even servants, sign the Mayflower Compact. Although the agreement was a step toward giving everyone an equal say in decisions, no women were allowed to sign it. Women had no voice in government at the time.

The Mayflower Compact

In spite of being in the wrong place, the Scrooby Separatists decided to stay. Because they were not on the London Company's land, they would not be under the company's laws and regulations. Realizing there would be a need for some form of law and order, three Separatist leaders—William Brewster, William Bradford, and Edward Winslow—proposed a simple agreement to govern the colony.

This agreement came to be called the "Mayflower Compact" and called for a **civil** government. It would not be an independent government, however, as the group recognized that they were still under the rule of the English king. Forty-one of the men signed the compact and elected John Carver, one of the original agents, to serve as the first governor of the colony.

The Mayflower Compact

"In ye name of God Amen. We whose names are underwriten, the loyal subjects of our dread Soveraigne Lord King James, by ye grace of God, of great Britaine, France and Ireland king, defender of the faith, etc.

"Haveing undertaken, for ye glorie of God, and advancemente of ye Christian faith, and honour of our king and countrie, a voyage to plant ye first colonie in the Northerne parts of Virginia, doe by these presents solemnly and mutualy in the presence of God, and one of another, covenant and combine ourselves togeather into a civill body politick, for our better ordering, and preservation and furtherance of ye ends aforesaid; and by vertue herof to enacte, constitute, and frame such just and equal lawes, **ordinances**, Acts, constitutions, and offices, from time to time, as shall be thought most meete and convenient for ye generall good of ye colonie: unto which we promise all due submission and obedience. In witnes wherof we have hereunder subscribed our names at Cape-Cod ye 11 of November, in ye year of ye raigne of our soveraigne Lord King James of England, France, and Ireland ye eighteenth, and of Scotland ye fiftie fourth. Ano: dom. 1620. "

The text of the Mayflower Compact as recorded by William Bradford,
Of Plimoth Plantation 1620–1647. *The original document has been lost.*

The landing on Cape Cod gave the travelers their first chance to get off the ship. In this picture, women wash clothes and cook while the men in the background train with their weapons.

The *Mayflower* captain and passengers knew where they were because they carried John Smith's map of New England. John Smith was a colonist from Jamestown, Virginia, who had explored the North American coast in 1614.

The First Days

While exploration parties searched the coast around Cape Cod Bay for a place to build a village, many of the colonists—still on board the *Mayflower*—were falling seriously ill from **scurvy** and pneumonia. Food supplies were low, and from the second day of their arrival, the travelers stole food and other supplies from Native dwellings, grain stores, and even graves. They didn't meet any of the people they were stealing from, since the Native people ran away from them. William Bradford recorded that they struggled with their consciences before taking things, but the Separatists generally viewed their actions as taking advantage of opportunities sent by God. In spite of these "special providences," however, four people had died by the middle of December.

Finding Plymouth Harbor

During their explorations for a good village site, several men in a small boat were caught in a storm in early December 1620. They rowed toward what looked like a space between two outcroppings of land. The tide caught the boat and carried it to shore, and the men found themselves in a protected natural harbor. It was deep and large enough to hold several ships.

When the men explored the land nearby, they discovered a freshwater river running into the harbor and cleared fields ready for planting. Large forests were close enough to provide firewood and building material. They had found Patuxet, now deserted after the recent death of its Native inhabitants from an epidemic.

The explorers returned to their ship. When they described the harbor they had found to Captain Jones of the *Mayflower*, he was able to locate the spot on the map of New England drawn by John Smith from his expedition in 1614. Smith had presented his map to King James I, who had given English names to many locations. Patuxet had already been renamed by the king as New Plymouth before the *Mayflower* arrived in New England, and Plymouth was the name the settlers adopted for their colony.

Within three days, the *Mayflower* set off for the final leg of its journey. On December 16, it was anchored in Plymouth Bay.

The passengers from the *Mayflower* finally go ashore at the site that will become their settlement. Like all known images of the first Plymouth settlers, this drawing was done much later—in this case, about 1830—and is the product of an artist's imagination.

Chapter 4

Settling at Plymouth

The colonists started building their settlement in deep winter. Their first task, before building individual homes, was to build a large common house for general use and storage.

A Hard Winter

With a location chosen at last, the settlers began building their village. Most of them slept on the *Mayflower*, as there was no housing for them, but came ashore daily to work.

The settlers planned to build a house for each family and to assign the single men to live with the families. But by this time, many settlers were seriously ill and dying. January and February 1621 were the hardest months, and in that time, just six or seven of the colonists remained healthy. They did everything they could to take care of the others, but by March, only twenty-five men, eight women, and twenty children were still alive out of the original one hundred or so passengers.

There were deaths among the sailors of the *Mayflower* as well. These were fewer, however, because they were more used to the hardships of sea voyages and because the captain kept separate food supplies for himself and his crew.

Samoset

During this time, the settlers had had no direct contact with any Native people who lived in the area. In March 1621, however, a man walked out of the woods and greeted the settlers. His name was Samoset—a sachem from the Abenaki people of what is now Maine—and he was in the area on a hunting trip. Samoset had learned to speak English from sailors who crossed the Atlantic to fish along the New England shores. The next time he returned, he told the starving settlers to expect a visit from Chief Massasoit, the grand sachem of the Wampanoag, who lived 40 miles (64 kilometers) away in Narragansett Bay.

A Visit from Samoset

"And whilst we were busied hereabout . . . there presented himself a savage, which caused an alarm. . . . He was a tall straight man, the hair of his head black, long behind, only short before, none on his face at all; he asked some beer, but we gave him strong water and biscuit, and butter, and cheese, and pudding, and a piece of mallard. . . . He told us the place where we now live is called Patuxet, and that about four years ago all the inhabitants died of an extraordinary plague. . . . All the afternoon we spent in communication with him. . . . We lodged him that night at Stephen Hopkin's house, and watched him. The next day he went away back to the Massasoits . . . who are our next bordering neighbors."

Edward Winslow and William Bradford, Mourt's Relation, *an account of Plymouth in 1620 and 1621, published in 1622*

This engraving shows Samoset's arrival at the Plymouth colony in the spring of 1621. It was probably something of a surprise to the colonists, who had had no contact with any people in the region.

When Massasoit arrived to visit the new inhabitants of his chiefdom, he brought with him sixty warriors as a show of his power.

The Arrival of Massasoit

Four or five days later, Chief Massasoit arrived. Massasoit had many good reasons to hate the Europeans. He knew of instances where Europeans had stolen from and cheated his people and had killed those who were only protecting their homes and hunting grounds. In spite of this, Massasoit decided to try and establish peace with these Europeans. He may have done so because he needed an ally against the Massachuset—the Wampanoag's enemy—and the Narragansett, who had become the strongest group in the area since the epidemics. Another reason for his friendliness could have been that the French—who had colonies to the north in what are now Maine and Canada—had allied themselves with enemies of the Wampanoag and were giving weapons to these groups. Massasoit may well have hoped to acquire weapons from the English. Whatever the reason, the Wampanoag and the colonists worked out an alliance. They agreed not to harm each other, and if either group was attacked, they would go to one another's defense.

Squanto and Survival

Massasoit had brought with him a Patuxet man named Tisquantum, or Squanto as the settlers came to call him. Squanto had been kidnapped from his village and was in England at the time the epidemic struck his village. Thus he had become the only known survivor of Patuxet. When Chief Massasoit left, Squanto remained in Plymouth. In the spring of 1621, he taught the colonists many survival skills, including how to plant and **fertilize** corn and how to fish. Since fish were plentiful, they were used as fertilizer in the cornfields. The fish were buried in the soil where corn was sown.

Squanto (c. 1585–1622)

Squanto lived in Patuxet, now in Massachusetts, until 1614, when he and about twenty other young Wampanoag men were kidnapped by English sailors intending to sell them as slaves. Squanto was sold to a Catholic monastery in Spain. He spent about two years there and then went to England, where he worked for the family of John Slanie, a merchant. In 1618 or 1619, Slanie helped arrange for Squanto to travel back to America. When Squanto arrived at his village, he found the entire community wiped out by an epidemic. He stayed with other Wampanoag groups until he came back to live at Patuxet in 1621 and help the new colony of Plymouth. Squanto served as an interpreter between his people and the colony until he became sick and died in 1622.

Squanto demonstrates Wampanoag farming methods to the Plymouth colonists.

A reconstruction of Hobomok's longhouse stands at Plimoth Plantation. Longhouses ranged from 60 to 80 feet (19 to 24 m) in length and were about 20 feet (6 m) wide. Strips of bark covered the sides like shingles. In winter, a second layer of bark helped keep the home warm.

As the weather grew warmer, the colonists grew healthier. Under Squanto's direction, they planted 20 acres (8 hectares) with corn and 6 acres (2.4 ha) with barley and peas. They then started vegetable gardens. The settlers were able to build better housing, and things started to look hopeful.

Hobomok

Another Wampanoag man, Hobomok, soon came to live at Plymouth. At first, the colonists weren't sure if he was a spy or a friend, but they took him in. There was some jealousy between Squanto and Hobomok, but both men were very helpful, and Hobomok stayed for many years.

Bradford Becomes Governor

The *Mayflower* had stayed through the winter, but on April 5, 1621, it set sail for England. Captain Jones offered to take back any of the colonists who wanted to leave, but none accepted his offer.

On June 1, 1621, the Council for New England issued a grant to Plymouth Colony. It gave the colonists official permission to stay where they were. That summer, Governor John Carver died of

William Bradford (1590–1657)

William Bradford was born in in Yorkshire, England. He was a devout Puritan, and at the age of twelve, he began attending the Separatist church at Scrooby. When the Scrooby Separatists emigrated to Holland in 1608, Bradford went with them, emerging as a church leader at the age of eighteen. He was elected Plymouth's governor in 1621 and was reelected thirty times, serving every year except five until 1656. Over many years, he wrote his journal *Of Plimoth Plantation 1620–1647*, which became the most important historical source of information about the settling of Plymouth.

The first page of William Bradford's
Of Plimoth Plantation 1620–1647.

sunstroke, and William Bradford was elected to be the new governor. He continued to forge a strong relationship with the Wampanoag and sent men to defend Massasoit when his leadership was threatened.

The harvest of 1621 was not large, but the settlers knew they would not starve that winter. The colonists and the Wampanoag organized a harvest celebration sometime between late September and early November. Their alliance was reaffirmed by the joint celebration, but once again the Wampanoag made a show of strength. Massasoit brought ninety warriors, considerably outnumbering the fifty or so colonists in Plymouth.

A garden was planted at the side of each house in Plymouth as soon as it was built because the food grown there was as important as the shelter itself. This garden at Plimoth Plantation contains the same vegetables, herbs, and medicinal plants that the colonists grew.

Rejoicing and Feasting

"Our harvest being gotten in, our governor sent four men on **fowling**, that so we might after a special manner rejoice together after we had gathered the fruit of our labors. They four in one day killed as much fowl as, with a little help beside, served the company almost a week. At which time, among other recreations, we exercised our arms, many of the Indians coming amongst us, and among the rest their greatest king Massasoit, with some ninety men, whom for three days we entertained and feasted. . . ."

Colonist Edward Winslow, in a letter of December 1621

A Harvest Feast

On arrival, Massasoit sent his men to hunt for deer and provided other foods, too. The colonists probably served various wildfowl, fish, stewed pumpkin, and cornmeal. The Wampanoag stayed for three days.

The winter of 1621 was not so severe, with less illness and fewer deaths, although the arrival of new settlers meant there were more mouths to feed. In addition, the investors in England were demanding goods in return for their investment. The colonists loaded a ship with timber and furs, but the cargo was stolen by French pirates during the ship's journey to England. Paying the investors would continue to be a problem for several years.

The Thanksgiving Holiday

In Native American society and in England, harvest ceremonies, such as the one held in 1621 and pictured below, were common in most farming communities. But the custom has nothing to do with the present Thanksgiving Day, which originated from a Puritan tradition of gathering to thank God when things were going well at any time of the year. (The Plymouth settlers held their first thanksgiving in 1623, after a drought.)

The Puritan thanksgiving tradition was adopted as an annual event by many New Englanders in the eighteenth century. The first national thanksgiving holiday was declared by the United States in 1777. The tradition did not last, although it was revived periodically. Not until 1863, when President Lincoln issued a proclamation for a day of thanksgiving, did the holiday become an annual, national event. The Plymouth connection was introduced later in the nineteenth century, and in the early 1900s, the holiday and the Pilgrims really became connected. The day and date varied until 1941, when the fourth Thursday of November was declared Thanksgiving Day.

Chapter 5

Life in Plymouth Colony

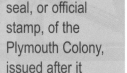

This is the first seal, or official stamp, of the Plymouth Colony, issued after it acquired its legal status in 1621.

Government and Religion Intertwined

The patent that had been given to the Plymouth Colony by the Council for New England in 1621 gave settlers the right to self-government. As the colony established itself, a form of government emerged. The men who made the rules—no women had political power at the time—were Separatists, even though they were not the majority group of settlers.

The Separatists were so powerful because only **freemen** could decide laws, and freemen had to be members of the Separatist church. The freemen were those who had signed the Mayflower Compact plus a few other original settlers who had since proved their worth. They had rights that other male colonists did not have: they elected the governor and sat in the General Court that made and administered laws.

Strict and Simple Laws

Although the Separatists had come in search of religious freedom, they did not practice it where other religions were concerned. **Quakers**, for instance, were excluded from government, and Native American religions were considered unacceptable.

The laws were simple but strict, and many were derived from the settlers' Puritan beliefs. Length of hair, smoking, and dancing were all moral issues that were controlled by laws, and lawbreakers were punished with fines, work, or public humiliation in the **stocks**.

Change of Ownership

After 1623, the Plymouth government allowed the colonists each to farm an acre (0.4 ha) plot of their own, instead of farming the land **communally**. In 1627, a bigger change was made. The colony's leaders made an agreement with the investors to buy their share of Plymouth. The houses, land, and livestock were then divided between about fifty-five male settlers who were freemen. A group of eight to twelve freemen, led by Governor Bradford, took personal responsibility for the colony's debt. In exchange, the group would run and receive all the profits from the colony's fur trade.

Plymouth Village

The original town of Plymouth was built on the side of a hill, with a wide street running east to west through its center. By the fall of 1621, the colonists had probably built seven houses and four buildings for storehouses and general use. Each family had its own fenced garden plot.

A picture from 1891 gives one artist's idea of how Plymouth looked in 1622, with the fort at the top of the hill on the right. The picture probably makes the village appear more spacious, well kept, and comfortable than it really was.

The first houses in Plymouth were were made of planks of wood over a timber frame and looked like this one being constructed in Plimoth Plantation. They were covered with thatched (woven straw) roofs, which were later replaced with wooden roofs to reduce fire danger.

In 1622, the whole of the town was enclosed with a **palisade**. That June—after news arrived of an Indian attack on the settlement at Jamestown, Virginia, that had resulted in many deaths—the settlers also started building a fort on top of the hill, where a watch could be kept. Until a church was built in 1648, the fort was also where the community worshiped. By 1624, there were about 180 people and 32 houses in Plymouth.

A Child's Life

Children in Plymouth had to do whatever they were old enough to manage, and they worked much harder than children do today. Like everyone else, they labored in the fields. They also fetched water, dug for **groundnuts** and other edible roots, and tended animals. There was no school in the early years, although children were given some schooling at home and at church. Even without school, there was little time to play, since every day except Sunday was a work day, and Sundays were for worship. When they could, however, children played marbles or ball games and running games.

Everyday Survival

Daily life in early Plymouth was taken up with activities necessary for survival. The people had to work hard just to feed themselves, although the **Sabbath** (observed on Sunday by Christians) was sacred, and no one worked or played that day.

Raising crops was the most important activity for everyone. The cornfields were fertilized with fish caught from the nearby river in an ingenious fashion. The villagers had constructed a system of sliding doors that trapped the fish in a pond as they swam upstream but let the water run through. The fish were then scooped into baskets and deposited into cornfields.

There was some livestock farming after 1624, but in the early years, hunting was the main source of meat. The men also cleared land, chopped firewood, and took turns on guard duty at night. The women cooked, sewed, made household goods, and took care of children. Servants lived with the family. Although they took orders and were sometimes poorly treated, they worked alongside family members rather than doing their work for them.

For a time, the original fort doubled as a church and meeting house. Attending services of worship was an important part of Plymouth's everyday life.

The interior of this house at Plimoth Plantation is typical of the early days of the colony. The houses had one main room with a fireplace and a small upstairs loft. There were few windows, and the floors consisted of packed earth.

Plentiful Food

Food was surprisingly good and plentiful in Plymouth Colony, considering that the settlers had come so close to starvation. There was abundant seafood of all kinds, and eels were a particular favorite. Like the Wampanoag, the colonists preserved fish and game by drying and smoking it so that it could be stored for times when food was scarce. Once cattle were introduced, the settlers had milk and beef. Colonists learned from the Wampanoag which wild plants were edible, and the woods also held many kinds of wildfowl, at

Soap Making

The settlers at Plymouth, like other Europeans of the seventeenth century, believed bathing was unhealthy and hardly ever washed. They did, however, need some soap for the few occasions they washed their clothes and themselves. Soap making was one of the women's many tasks. First they made lye, a by-product of wood ash, by pouring water over ashes from the fire. The water dripped through, drawing with it a substance called potash, which has cleaning properties. The potash was boiled to make it more concentrated and turn it into lye. The liquid lye was then used as a powerful cleaning agent (like bleach) or mixed with animal fats to make a soapy paste.

least until their numbers decreased with the growth of the human population.

Making Everything

For the first twenty years, few skilled craftspeople lived in Plymouth. Carpenters, leather tanners, boat builders, and blacksmiths were all in short supply. As a result, the Plymouth settlers had very few material possessions, even compared to other groups of the same period. Some metal tools and glassware had come from England, but nearly everything in the colony had to be made by hand. From soap and candles to barrels and farm tools, the colonists had to produce those necessities that they had not brought with them.

Within the community, an **economy** of sorts developed based on an exchange of services and products, similar to bartering systems in English villages. People did not have money, and so they paid each other by exchanging their labor. For instance, a load of firewood could be exchanged for the services of a miller to grind grain or for a pair of shoe soles.

Samplers were sewn by girls and women to record different needlework stitches and designs. This one from 1653 is the earliest known sampler made in America. It is the work of Loara, daughter of Plymouth's military leader Myles Standish.

Industry and Commerce

In 1622, the Plymouth colonists began to trade for necessities from outside the colony. In exchange for tools, weapons, and trinkets—such as chains, mirrors, and glass beads—they would acquire grain and meat for their colony from the Wampanoag.

As the colony became stable, its trade rapidly expanded to include furs and other items that could be sent to England. By 1625, the colonists were trading for animal hides, making regular trips to Native groups in present-day Maine to acquire furs. Fur, especially beaver, was in great demand in Europe. A system of **currency** using wampum—pieces of shell from clams or sea snails—evolved between Native groups and white settlers.

Plymouth set up two fur trading posts in what is now Maine, on the Penobscot and Kennebec Rivers. In the 1630s, Plymouth's trading network also extended south as far

These furs are drying in the recreated Hobomok's longhouse at Plimoth Plantation. Indians dried the hides before selling them to white traders, and the furs were then packed in barrels and sent to England.

as New Amsterdam (now New York). By that time, in addition to trading with Native peoples for fur, Plymouth colonists were selling cattle and grain to new settlers.

Plymouth Colony Grows

In 1630, Plymouth received a new patent that defined its boundaries. The patent also granted the colony land on the Kennebec River, now in Maine, where it had set up a fur-trading post.

By the early 1630s, the colony had begun to spread. People left to form new settlements, the first being Duxbury across Plymouth Bay. Soon there were other communities, such as Scituate, Barnstable, and Yarmouth. By 1640, Plymouth Colony had expanded to eight towns and 2,500 people, and the original village of Plymouth was just a small part of a diverse colony.

These boundaries were set by the 1630 patent given to the Plymouth Colony. The patent included Cape Cod, and new communities soon appeared there.

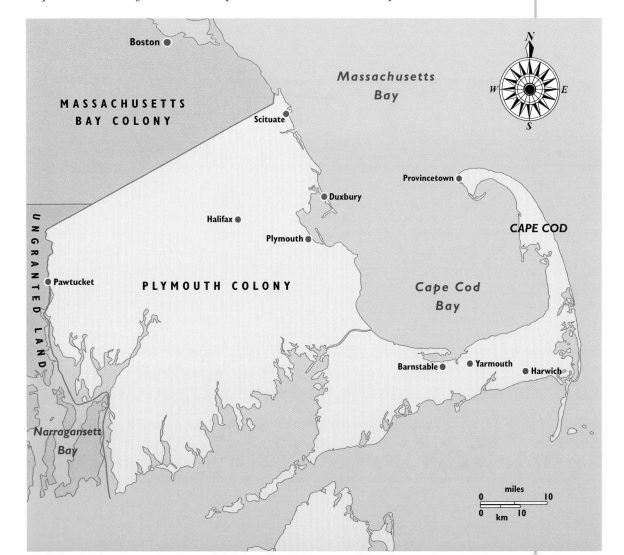

Puritan Expansion

Arrival of the Puritans

In the late 1620s, another group of English Puritans emigrated to New England. They were not Separatists, and there were several differences between the Plymouth settlers and these new immigrants. Most were well educated and fairly wealthy. They were also idealists and had a vision of building a society wholly devoted to God. Although the Separatists believed that theirs was the right way to worship God, they weren't too concerned about converting others. This new group of Puritans intended to set an example that the whole world could see and follow.

A view of Boston, Massachusetts, in its very earliest days as the center of Massachusetts Bay Colony.

The Massachusetts Bay Colony

Between June 1628 and March 1630, more than eight hundred Puritan settlers arrived in Massachusetts Bay, just north of Plymouth. The new colony was extremely well planned, very well supplied, and adequately financed. The Puritan leaders in London selected John Winthrop, a wealthy man who was deeply committed to Puritan ideas, to govern the new colony.

The community settled on the Shawmut peninsula, where they built a village they named Boston. The basic laws that were to govern the colony were determined by investors in London. But the church did not have to answer to any central authority, and it really ruled the community. All citizens were required to attend church services. If they did not, they were punished. All were required to give part of their income for the support of the church. From 1647, any Massachusetts Bay community of fifty or more families was required to open a school and support it with taxes.

The Massachusetts Bay Colony rapidly became the dominant white settlement in New England. Between 1630 and 1643, about two hundred ships came to the colony, bringing twenty thousand new colonists. The colony expanded into towns all over the Bay area and into the area that would become Connecticut, where an epidemic had killed most of the Indian population.

Resistance to Puritan Control

At first, it seemed the Puritans would manage to set up the kind of society they had dreamed of. But as Massachusetts Bay Colony grew and the people moved ever farther from Boston, the Puritan leaders lost control of them. Industry and commerce took hold, and by the 1650s, trade was an important part of life.

The Puritans valued education highly because people needed to be educated to read the Bible. In 1635, they started the first public school in the colonies. In 1638, the Puritans opened the first college, Harvard University, shown here in the 1730s.

Quakers, who first arrived in Boston in 1656, were imprisoned, persecuted and expelled by the Puritans. Those who refused to leave could be punished by death. This scene shows Quaker men being whipped as they are paraded through the street.

Many people disagreed with the Puritan ideas on which the colony's government was based. On June 1, 1660, Mary Dyer was hanged for the "crime" of being a Quaker. This upset a lot of people who thought their leaders had gone too far.

In 1636, a Puritan teacher named Roger Williams fled the Massachusetts area to avoid arrest for his views. He set up a new colony in what would become Rhode Island. The colony practiced freedom of religion and instituted a form of democracy that allowed all free males a vote in the government.

Roger Williams (c. 1603–1683)

Roger Williams was born in London and attended Cambridge University, where he became committed to Puritanism. Williams emigrated to Massachusetts in 1631 and soon came into disagreement with church authorities because he thought they should break entirely from the Church of England. Williams also stated that the king had no right to give the land in Massachusetts to anyone because it belonged to the Indians and that church authorities should not have the right to punish people for not going to church. In 1636, the authorities ordered his arrest and deportation to England, but Williams escaped to what is now the state of Rhode Island. Other rebels followed him, and they established the first colony with true freedom of religion and complete separation of church and state. Williams was a leader in that colony until his death.

During this time, there was little contact between Plymouth and Massachusetts Bay except for trade, although some people who found Massachusetts too rigid fled to Plymouth. The Plymouth leaders did not always agree with the policies of their neighboring colony, but there were no open conflicts.

Relations with Native People

Relations with the original inhabitants of New England had grown steadily worse ever since the arrival of the Massachusetts Bay colonists. The Puritans assumed they and their culture were superior in every way and considered the Indians as little better than animals. The overwhelming numbers of the settlers and their more advanced weapons enabled Puritans to force people off land that they wanted for themselves.

Not only did the Puritans take the Native people's land, piece by piece and year by year, but they also attempted to stamp out their religion. About four thousand Native people in New England became Christians, but the majority of Wampanoags, Narragansetts, and Massachusets had no desire to adopt English ways. Some were forced by the Puritans into what they called praying towns, basically labor camps where Native religions and customs were banned.

Roger Williams is greeted by Native Americans as he arrives at Rhode Island.

King Philip's War

During the lifetime of Massasoit and that of his successor Wamsutta, the peace was kept with the Wampanoag at least. But Wamsutta died in 1662 and was succeeded by his brother, Metacom, or King Philip. King Philip realized that he would have to fight to keep any land at all for his people. In 1675, after persuading other groups in New England to form an alliance with the Wampanoag, he went to war.

Metacom, or King Philip, as he was known, united the Native groups of New England in a last effort against the white settlers who had taken their land and devastated their population.

Massasoit (c. 1580—1661)

Massasoit was born about 1580 and was the sachem of the Wampanoag people during the early years of Puritan settlement. In *Mourt's Relation* he is described as "a very [healthy] man, in his best years, an able body, grave of countenance, and spare of speech. In his attire little or nothing differing from the rest of his followers, only in a great chain of white bone beads about his neck . . . his face was painted with a sad red . . . and oiled both head and face, that he looked greasily."

The relationship between the Wampanoag and Plymouth grew strong under Massasoit's leadership, but problems arose when other, non-Separatist, Puritans arrived in large numbers. Tribal authority disintegrated as lands and traditions disappeared, and even Massasoit adopted English ways. He renamed his son Wamsutta Alexander and his son Metacom Philip. Massasoit was succeeded after his death by Wamsutta, who was succeeded by his brother Metacom.

At first, King Philip's men staged successful raids and won their conflicts with the colonists. But eventually the colonists adapted to Native methods of fighting, and their sheer numbers overwhelmed the Indians. In August 1676, the colonists captured and executed King Philip, and by 1677, the last resistance was gone. Hostility increased toward the greatly reduced Indian population of southern New England, however, and the colonial governments placed great restrictions on Native life. In addition, until the the early 1700s, Native Americans in New England were often forced into slavery by white colonists.

The town of Brookfield, Massachusetts, is attacked by Native Americans during King Philip's War. The war lasted from 1675 to 1677. Hundreds of settlers and thousands of Native people died in the conflict.

Conclusion

A ship called the *Mayflower II* was built in England using authentic seventeenth-century materials. The recreated ship was then sailed to Plymouth in 1957.

Royal Colonies

In 1685, both Massachusetts and Plymouth lost their unusual independence when King James II appointed a royal governor for New England. On October 17, 1691, a royal charter declared Plymouth to be part of Massachusetts. The region of Massachusetts remained a British colony until the colonies declared their independence in 1776.

Plymouth Today

Each year, about one million people visit Plymouth's historical places such as Burial Hill, the site of one of the first forts built by the Pilgrims. The hill also has a graveyard where William Bradford and other early settlers are buried. Plymouth boasts more than a dozen museums, including a Pilgrim wax museum and a children's museum. Pilgrim Hall Museum is the oldest museum in continuous operation in the United States. It houses most of the few Plymouth artifacts that have been found.

Plimoth Plantation is a living history museum that has a reconstruction of the village as it was in 1627. The village contains houses, the fort, pens for livestock, gardens, and fields for crops, all of which are maintained and worked just as the colonists would have done. The buildings and artifacts are as true to the originals as possible. Hobomok's homesite nearby is a recreation of a typical Wampanoag dwelling.

The *Mayflower II*

The *Mayflower II* is part of Plimoth Plantation but is located at a separate site about 3 miles (5 km) away, near Plymouth Rock in the harbor. It is a full-scale reproduction of a seventeenth-century merchant ship of the same type as the *Mayflower*. Visitors to the ship can learn the story of the original voyage and the settlers' first winter, when most of them lived on the *Mayflower*.

It is unlikely that the *Mayflower* passengers chose Plymouth Rock (left) as a convenient spot to disembark, but the myth has existed since 1741. In 1774, an effort was made to move Plymouth Rock to the town square, but the rock split in two, and only half of it was moved. That half was then moved to Pilgrim Hall in 1834 before being reunited with the bottom half in 1880.

The Legacy of Plymouth

The Separatists among the colonists at Plymouth came to America to found a colony where they would be free to practice their religion, which they felt was the only right and true one. The idea of true religious freedom—which means that people are free to worship as they choose—appeared in later colonies in New England and was written into the Constitution of the United States of America. The first of the Plymouth settlers are sometimes known as the "Founding Fathers" because the first English colonies in North America are considered by some people to be the foundation on which the United States of America was built.

Time Line

1606	Scrooby Separatists form own church.
1608	Scrooby Separatists emigrate to Amsterdam.
1609	Scrooby Separatists move to Leiden, Netherlands.
1614	John Smith explores and maps New England.
1617	Epidemic kills inhabitants of Patuxet village.
1620	February: Scrooby Separatists receive a patent from Virginia Company of London to settle in Virginia.
	August 5: *Mayflower* and *Speedwell* make first attempt at departure.
	September 16: *Mayflower* sets sail alone for North America.
	November 11: *Mayflower* anchors in present-day Provincetown Harbor, and Mayflower Compact is drawn up.
	November 13: King James I grants charter for New England to Council for New England.
	December 10: Explorers find Plymouth Harbor.
	December 16: *Mayflower* anchors at Plymouth Harbor.
1621	March 16: Samoset visits Plymouth Colony.
	March: Massasoit visits Plymouth Colony, bringing Squanto.
	April: *Mayflower* returns to England.
	Summer: Plymouth governor John Carver dies, and William Bradford is elected governor.
	Fall: Plymouth settlers and Wampanoag hold harvest celebration.
	November: More settlers arrive from England.
1622	November: Squanto dies.
1623	April: Colonists switch from communal farming to individual plots.
1627	Colonists buy out London investors.
1630	New patent defines Plymouth boundaries.
	Massachusetts Bay Colony is founded.
1636	Roger Williams founds Rhode Island Colony.
1657	William Bradford dies.
1661	Chief Massasoit dies and is succeeded by Wamsutta.
1662	Wamsutta dies and is succeeded by Metacom (King Philip).
1675–1677	King Philip's War.
1691	October 17: Plymouth becomes part of Massachusetts.

Glossary

civil: to do with citizens and ordinary people rather than religious or military affairs or authorities.

colony: settlement, area, or country owned or controlled by another nation.

communal: something owned or done as a group rather than for individual benefit.

compact: agreement.

confederacy: alliance of groups that agree to act together and support each other.

constitution: basic rules of government for a nation.

cooper: person who makes barrels.

currency: anything used as a unit of exchange.

dissenter: person who disagrees with and sometimes acts against the accepted beliefs of his or her society.

economy: system of producing and distributing goods and services.

epidemic: rapid spread of disease that affects large number of people.

fertilize: add substances to soil to make it better for growing plants.

fowling: hunting and killing wildfowl.

freeman: originally one of the forty-one signers of the Mayflower Compact. The number of freemen slowly increased in Plymouth, however, as other reliable men applied to be and were accepted as freemen.

groundnut: plant with an edible root.

indentured servant: worker who agrees to work for a set period of time in exchange for an opportunity offered by an employer.

ordinance: local rule or law.

palisade: wooden fence made of large, pointed stakes.

patent: exclusive right to use or earn money from something.

pilgrim: person who goes on a religious journey. Also used to mean the early journey. Also European colonists in North America.

Puritan: person belonging to a Protestant Christian group that wanted to purify the Church of England. The word has since come to describe a person with very strict moral codes.

Quaker: person belonging to a Christian group that has no ministers, rejects church rituals, and opposes all wars and violence.

Sabbath: day of rest and worship.

scurvy: disease, resulting from a lack of vitamin C in the diet, that causes soft gums, loose teeth, and bleeding.

Separatist: person belonging to a Puritan group that separated from the Church of England.

stocks: device for punishing people. A person's head and hands are placed through holes in a wooden structure and locked into place. The person is then left for a long period of time.

Further Information

Books

Bradford, William and Margaret Wise Brown (Editor). *Homes in the Wilderness: A Pilgrim's Journal of Plymouth Plantation in 1620*. Linnet Books, 1988.

Bruchac, Joseph. *Squanto's Journey*. Silver Whistle, 2000.

Erickson, Paul. *Daily Life in the Pilgrim Colony 1636*. Clarion Books, 2001.

Grace, Catherine O'Neill. *1621: A New Look at Thanksgiving*. National Geographic Society, 2001.

Lasky, Kathryn. *A Journey to the New World: The Diary of Remember Patience Whipple, Mayflower, 1620* (Dear America). Scholastic, 1996.

Sita, Lisa. *Indians of the Northeast: Traditions, History, Legends, and Life*. Gareth Stevens, 2000.

Web Sites

www.pilgrimhall.org Pilgrim Hall Museum has the largest collection of Plymouth artifacts, many of them shown here with interesting details about their use and owners.

www.plimoth.org Plimoth Plantation web site offers pictures of the reconstructed village plus plenty of good information about the first settlers, the Wampanoag, and the daily lives of both groups.

www.bostonkids.org/teachers/TC/ The Children's Museum, Boston, and the Wampanoag people offer a joint web site about Wampanoag culture and history.

Useful addresses

Plimoth Plantation
P. O. Box 1620
Plymouth, MA 02362
Telephone: (508) 746-1622

Index

Page numbers in *italics* indicate maps and diagrams. Page numbers in **bold** indicate other illustrations.